The American
Medical Mess

The American Medical Mess

By
Charles Peter

iUniverse, Inc.
New York Bloomington

iUniverse books may be ordered through booksellers or by contacting:

iUniverse
1663 Liberty Drive
Bloomington, IN 47403
www.iuniverse.com
1-800-Authors (1-800-288-4677)

ISBN: 978-1-4401-0679-8 (pbk)
ISBN: 978-1-4401-0680-4 (ebk)

Printed in the United States of America

iUniverse rev. date: 1/22/2009

Acknowledgment

For my grandfather, a country doctor and a president of the Florida Medical Association, who always feared socialized medicine, i.e. medicine run by the government. Seventy-five years later, his worst fears came to pass. Little did he dream that now the Insurance Cartel _is_ the government.

Preface

One does not need to read a book to know that American medicine is a mess. One has but to get sick or to buy medical insurance.

One trillion, seven hundred million to two trillion dollars is spend yearly in the United States on health care. If health care could be delivered efficiently and could be delivered without theft and fraud, the cost of medical care could be reduced by one third to one half.

There are approximately three hundred million people in the United States. If the average family is comprised of four members, Bruce and Bob notwithstanding, then there are seventy-five to eighty million families in the United States. If one third of two trillion dollars could be saved, a family of four would have over $250 a month to spend. Because corporations pay for most of the health insurance, they would be more competitive in world markets, and United States workers would not lose their jobs.

Mighty General Motors is near bankruptcy because General Motors agreed to furnish health insurance for its retired workers. Little did General Motors know how much the health care providers could steal. Fire Engine Charlie Wilson, General Motors president, said, "What's good for General Motors is good for the USA." Although vilified at the time for making the statement, his statement is still true today. Starbucks pays more for health insurance than it pays for coffee beans.

This book is written from the perspective of someone in Harris County (Houston) Texas. The facts and the thoughts contained herein may or may not be extrapolated to the rest of the country because, as we all know, everything in Texas is bigger and better ... bigger pollution, bigger lawsuits, bigger judgments and bigger thieves.

Ephraim McDowell

The following is excerpts from "The Life and Times of Ephraim McDowell" by Laman Gray, Sr. M.D., V.C. Reed & Sons, Printers, 1500 Arlington Ave, Lensville, KY 40506 – Date 1987.

In 1809, in Danville, Kentucky, of all places, Ephraim McDowell performed the first successful abdominal operation in which an organ was excised rather than incised. To put things in perspective, the country was founded in 1776, ether was not used until 1846, Lister had not developed his method of antisepsis until 1865, and Louis Pasteur's discoveries of bacterial cause of infection was not evolved until more than two generations later.

Ephraim McDowell was a scholarly young man, whose father was an influential politician and judge in Danville, Kentucky. At that time, one became a doctor through apprenticeship. After two years apprenticeship with Dr. Humphrey in Virginia, young McDowell studied two years at the University of Edinburgh, Scotland, the best medical school in the world at that time.

Young Ephraim returned to Danville, Kentucky to become the preeminent surgeon in the area. In 1809, fourteen years after he began the practice of medicine and then 38 years of age, he was requested to see Mrs. Jane Todd Crawford in Green County, Kentucky, some sixty miles from Danville, in the dead of winter.

Two local doctors thought that Mrs. Crawford was pregnant with twins and that she could not deliver. Dr. McDowell was called. After a horseback ride of sixty miles, Dr. McDowell examined Mrs. Crawford and concluded that she had a large ovarian cyst. He told Mrs. Crawford that if she were prepared to die, he would attempt an experimental operation and he would try to remove her tumor. She, however, would have to travel to Danville.

Because of her excruciating pain, this she did, bouncing her large ovarian tumor on the saddle horn for the entire sixty mile trip.

On a Sunday, in order that the churchgoers could pray for them, Dr. McDowell operated on Mrs. Crawford.

Because there was no anesthesia at the time, the patient probably received Laudanum (tincture of opium). Dr. McDowell made a nine inch incision, evacuated the gelatinous material from the cyst, tied a waxed string around the blood vessels and fallopian tube and removed the cyst. The operation took twenty-five minutes.

Mrs. Crawford survived and went home twenty-five days later. Dr. McDowell succeeded in part because he was a devotee of personal cleanliness, because he turned the patient on her side to let out the blood from her abdomen, because he washed her intestines with warm water and because he brought out the incision the ligatures around the blood vessels – this acted as a drain that removed any remaining blood and serum that would act as a culture medium for bacteria. The prayers didn't hurt.

Rumor had it that several of the town folks had assembled to lynch the good doctor if his operation failed – ancestors of our modern day plaintiff lawyers no doubt.

Today, if Mrs. Crawford wanted her ovarian cyst removed: The excruciating pain sends her to the emergency room of the local hospital where she waits seven hours to see an emergency room doctor, whose native tongue, most likely is not English. The average wait in the emergency rooms of Harris County Texas (Houston) is seven hours, unless you go to the Eleemosynary hospital, Ben Taub or LBJ (Lynden Baines Johnson) where the average wait is seventeen hours.

Before Mrs. Crawford gets to see the emergency room doctor, she sees the triage nurse. Then she is put into an examining room where she awaits the emergency room physician. There is another considerable wait because the emergency room physicians are paid by the hour and they seem to have little interest in expediting emergency room treatment.

On one occasion, the author came to see a patient in the emergency room. Many people were standing around because there were no more seats. I asked the nurse if one of the plants on the Ship Channel had blown up. She said no.

The next time that I came to the emergency room and there were a lot of people standing around, I said to the nurse, "The ER doctors are changing shifts." The nurse replied, "How did you know?" I replied, "Because it looks as if one of the plants on the Ship Channel blew up." Because they are paid by the hour, the ER doctors leave the patients for the next guy.

Finally, the emergency room doctor sees Mrs. Crawford. He immediately orders a pregnancy test, along with a blood count and blood chemistries. The pregnancy test must be done before a CT scan of the abdomen can be done. The ER doctor doesn't want a lawsuit twenty years from now because an unborn child did not get into Harvard Business School. One certainly does not want to x-ray a pregnant woman's fetus. This, along with fear of litigation causes pregnancy tests to be run on most all women.

Mrs. Crawford's pregnancy test is negative. A CT scan of the abdomen is done. The ER doctor calls Mrs. Crawford's family doctor to tell him that Mrs. Crawford has a large ovarian cyst but, Mrs. Crawford's doctor is in Las Vegas at a medical convention. He has checked out on a colleague. After another delay, the colleague calls and tells the ER doctor to give Mrs. Crawford a pain shot and to tell Mrs. Crawford to call her doctor in the morning. Her doctor is to be back in town tonight.

Mrs. Crawford leaves the emergency room and goes home. Her "wallet biopsy" cost several thousand dollars.

The next day, Mrs. Crawford calls her family doctor (now called her pcp – primary care physician or health care provider) for an appointment, but she can't be seen for another week. Mrs. Crawford can't go to see the gynecologist that will remove her ovarian cyst without first seeing her pcp/gatekeeper, even though he knows nothing about ovarian cysts. Mrs. Crawford has to make another visit to her pcp/gatekeeper to get a referral to a gynecologist.

Upon arriving at the gynecologist's office, the receptionist does another "green count" only to find out that the high school drop-out answering the telephone at the insurance company considers Mrs. Crawford's condition as being pre-existing. The gynecologist writes the medial director of the insurance company explaining Mrs. Crawford's condition.

The medical director relents and gives the gynecologist permission to treat Mrs. Crawford. The gynecologist reconsiders. "What if this thing is malignant? What if things don't go well?" he says to himself. "She will sue me. The plaintiff's lawyer will ask me, 'Well, Doctor, why didn't you send Mrs. Crawford to an oncological gynecologist?'"

Mrs. Crawford is referred to an oncological gynecologist (cancer surgeon) but the new doctor wants another referral, fearing that he/she won't be paid. Mrs. Crawford goes back to the pcp (primary care provider)'s office to get the necessary referral.

Finally, after a PAP smear, chest x-ray, ECG, CA-125 and a repeat of all of the lab tests done at her emergency room visit (more than two weeks had elapsed), Mrs. Crawford was scheduled for surgery.

Upon arriving at the hospital, Mrs. Crawford is given a ream of papers to fill out or to sign. It reminded her of when she refinanced her house.

The operation went well but it took a bit longer than the twenty-five minutes that it took Dr. McDowell to do the first one. In this operation, samples of the abdominal fluid were taken to see if any cancer cells were present. Perhaps a lymph node was biopsied.

The cyst was benign but post operatively, Mrs. Crawford ran fever, which was caused by atelectasis (incomplete expansion of the lung). Mrs. Crawford put out her last cigarette as she entered the hospital.

Mrs. Crawford's atelectasis responded to respiratory therapy but her hospital stay was longer than the three days authorized by her insurance carrier. This necessated the hospital calling the insurance company to get an extension of the original three days authorized. The "cookbook nurse" hired by the hospital to review charts found that this patient had fever and stayed in the hospital longer than allowed by her "cookbook". Because the patient had fever, the infection control nurse, hired by the hospital reviewed the chart. The chart was referred to the Ob-Gyn Committee. Another hospital employee prepared the chart for the Committee. Consultants in pulmonary medicine and infectious diseases were called in to see Mrs. Crawford because, if severe complications arose and Mrs. Crawford sued the oncological gynecologist, he would better be able to defend himself.

Mrs. Crawford was discharged from the hospital with a bill that made her gulp.

Almost two hundred years ago, Ephraim McDowell performed the same operation in twenty-five minutes with similar results. We can't go back to the days of Ephraim McDowell but certainly these operations could be done more efficiently.

Medicaid

In Texas a few years ago, Medicaid cost twenty-one billion dollars. This is about $600 per person living in Texas.

A recent newspaper article said that if the top twenty Medicaid fraud cases could be prosecuted to completion that seven hundred million dollars could be retrieved. What about the many thousand other cases.

Several years ago, Texas Medicaid was administered by the National Heritage Insurance Company (NHIC) which, I believe, was owned by Mr. Ross Perot. This worked well because all the doctor had to do was to take care of the patient, in or out of the hospital. But, alas, the doctors stole too much and Medicaid was turned over to the insurance oligarchs who put all of the Medicaid "entitlees" into HMOs (Health Maintenance Organizations) that kept the money and denied the Medicaid "entitlees" the health care for which they had been paid.

HMO Medicaid now pays so little that many doctors and hospitals won't treat Medicaid patients, resulting in Dr. McGuire's (CEO – United Health Care) administer of HMO Evercare-Nevercare of 1.7 billion dollars unexercised stock options.

Medicaid entitlees choose a primary care physician(PCP). To see a specialist, the entitlee must get a referral from his PCP. If the specialist thinks that the entitlee needs an operation, he may need to get permission from the HMO. Emergencies don't need prior authorization. Therefore, if a primary care physician (PCP) thinks that a patient needs hospitalization, he sends the patient to the emergency room to be admitted rather than await authorization from the HMO, resulting in an extra emergency room charge.

Due to the EMTALA Law (Emergency Medical Treatment and Active Labor Act) Medicare entitlees use emergency rooms as outpatient clinics and use ambulances as taxis.

A doctor sent a three year old Hispanic child to a speech therapist because the child did not put two English words together. No English was spoken at home and the TV was always on Telemundo or on Univision. It is a wonder that the child could speak one English word.

A peddler called and asked if I would sign an order for several items for a forty plus year old Cerebral Palsy patient, whose mother had taken excellent care of for all of his years. Before signing anything, I called the patient's mother who said, "I just wanted a new wheelchair because this one is worn out." I'm sure that if I had signed this order, the patient would have gotten a new wheelchair and the taxpayers would have gotten a bill for a number of undelivered items.

In front of a pawn shop in Houston there are a number of Medicare and Medicaid scooters.

Medicaid entitlees go to the emergency room with trivial complaints. It is free and the hospital's Fast Track or Satellite ERs are happy to take the taxpayers money.

If the Medicaid entitlee is displeased, he can complain to Medicaid and to the Texas Board of Medical Examiners. The following are two examples:

An ER doctor ordered a CT scan without contrast to evaluate a patient with suspected appendicitis. The Radiologist reported that the CT scan ruled out acute appendicitis. The ER doctor ordered another CT scan with contrast and the Radiologist refused to do it. When the Medicaid entitlee reported this to Medicaid and the Texas Board of Medical Examiners, people were sent to talk with the director of ER doctors, who told the inspectors that he could no more make a Radiologist do another CT scan than he could make a surgeon operate on a patient. The patient did not have appendicitis.

A patient with a positive pregnancy test had a normal ultrasound. The patient was told that it was too early to pick up a tubal pregnancy and that she should be admitted to the hospital for observation. The patient left against medical advice. A few days later, the patient went to the city-county hospital where she was told the same thing. Entitlee's husband/boyfriend complained and more inspectors were sent.

Mom and Dad bring child to the ER. Medicaid thinks that Mom is a single mom – she is not.

With regards to Medicaid entitlees, it appears that the tail is wagging the dog.

Doctors

Demean them, call them health care providers, try to replace them with nurses, but doctors are responsible for most health care expenditures. Doctors see patients, write prescriptions, put patients in the hospital, operate on patients and tell patients how often they should return for an office visit. Sometimes the interest of the doctor, the patient and the payer are not the same.

Most doctor's put their patient's interest first, some don't.

Workmen's Compensation laminectomies (disc operations, i.e. back operations) cost the health care system much money. Lately, the Workman's Compensation Insurance companies have been much less lenient in allowing laminectomies to be done.

Story has it that there were thirty green card Mexicans in a clean-up crew in a building about one mile from a plant explosion. Ten of them had lumbar laminectomies. The doctor's made money, the hospital made money, the lawyers made money and the patients retired in Mexico.

Many of these questionable laminectomies aren't simple disc removal operations. Some are two levels, spinal fusions with nuts and bolts. Workman's Compensation back operations (disc operations) have a much lower success rate than non-Workman's Compensation laminectomies. The Workman's Comp patients may need another back operation or epidural steroid injections (shots in the back). In Houston, there appears to be a sub-culture of people totally and permanently disabled from back operations.

The insurance cartel pays about $350 for a carpal tunnel operation, at which price the doctor loses money. A carpal tunnel operation is cutting the band on the front of the wrist. The band keeps the tendons from sticking out like a bowstring when the hand is moved down and sometimes the hand band gets too tight and compresses the median nerve (nerve to the hand muscles).

Not to be outdone, doctors began to do the operation with an endoscope and charging $3000. One doctor who advertises on TV had done over a thousand such operations. One might surmise that he operated on, everyone in the north side of the county who slept on his arm last night.

Two local doctors are now at Club Fed (minimum security federal prison) for getting kickbacks for writing prescriptions for wheel chairs. A newspaper article said that there was five hundred million dollars in wheelchair fraud on the Gulf Coast. One doctor in his late seventies was sentenced to eleven years. He probably irritated the judge when the first trial resulted in a hung jury. If he makes it that long the "Good Doctor" will get out of the joint when he is 90.

The Nigerian who put the scheme together fled to Nigeria with nine million dollars. The docs should have gone with him.

An employee told me that when her friend saw the gynecologist who told her that she had hemorrhoids and should see the proctologist downstairs. The proctologist (they want to be called colon and rectal surgeons now) wanted to operate on her hemorrhoids in 2-3 days. I asked if the hemorrhoids bled, clotted, hurt or protruded. The answer was, "no". I said, as a general rule, hemorrhoidectomies are done for bleeding or when the patient gets tired of them. Having ones entire behind clot might be another indication. The patient was asked to come in for a free evaluation. She had minimal or normal amount of hemorrhoids. You can bet that the proctologist is going to tell some patient that her womb is falling out and she should see the gynecologist upstairs.

Doctors have become limited partners in hospitals, usually to make money. Sometimes doctors become abused by private, church and government hospitals and want a better place to practice. When one large hospital was going to make all of the medical staff either be employed by the hospital or by the medical school, many of the doctors built their own hospital.

More likely the doctors join Ali Babba, the general partner, to make money. For their overutilization, the doctors receive their pittance every month while Ali Babba, the general partner, is farting through silk.

A newspaper reported that when some doctors draw blood in their office, that they not only charge for drawing the blood but also add a charge to what the lab charges.

Many patients need to come to the doctor's office frequently to get checked and to get their prescriptions refilled. Many don't. Some old patients come for a social visit with the doctor and his staff.

We now have a new specialist among us – the pain doctor. The pain doctor is usually an anesthesiologist who blocks nerves in an outpatient setting as well as dispense narcotics (through prescriptions) from his office. Some pain doctors can do 15-20 injections a morning in an outpatient facility. Much money can be made by the pain doctor and by the hospital or surgicenter. Insurance companies pay for the procedures because they think that hospital admissions are prevented. Pain doctors are a good place to dump patients who keep on complaining after surgery. A recent newspaper article suggested that many of the "street drugs" originated from pain doctors.

Whatever the government does is usually counter productive. The government came up to the IPA (Independent Physician's Association) to keep the patients well. The federal government gives the insurance company money to give to the IPA to take care of a number of patients – a certain amount of money per person, i.e. capitation. The doctors who own the IPA get paid, the doctors who run the IPA get paid and the doctors who take care of the patients get paid for each patient in the IPA. These are the same doctors. The primary care doctors see the patients first, then, if necessary, refer the patient to a specialist who is capitated (small amount for each patient in the panel). The doctors in the IPA were being paid to keep the patients well, but the doctors kept the money and denied treatment to the patients.

I saw a 46 year old man in the IPA who vomited blood for nine months before he was referred to a gastroenterologist who diagnosed his stomach cancer. The survival percentage for stomach cancer is not good, especially if one neglects the cancer for nine months. My colleague frequently told me of cancers that had advanced because diagnostic procedures weren't done. One primary care doctor didn't do routine mammograms on her patients,

The IPA signed up Medicare patients because the IPA paid for their drugs. These old people thought that this free medicine program was the greatest thing since Seven-Up. With a little thought, these people could have reasoned that they could not receive more than they were getting from the government if the government gave the same amount of money to the insurance company which took a whack out of it then gave money to the IPA who then took another whack out of it. Little did these old people realize that they were being denied care to which they were entitled, i.e. murdered.

Two older doctors were dropped from the HMO (Health Maintenance Organization) because they admitted two or three heart attack patients during a six month period. Older primary care doctors have older patients.

When HMOs first started, a primary care doctor put his patients in an HMO. The HMO kept the patients and fired the doctor – nice fellows, these insurance oligarchs.

Most doctors have their patient's interest first – some are businessmen.

The government got tired of the doctors and imported cheap foreign labor to bring down costs. Now, one third of the doctors in the country are from India. Most are excellent doctors, some are businessmen. In the Harris County Medical Roster, there are more Kims and Patels than there are Jones. The Jones are old.

Hospitals

Hospital charges are exorbitant. Hospital expenses are exorbitant in large part due to litigation (liability insurance) and to fear of liability (defensive medicine).

To provide better care and to avoid liability suits, hospitals hire infection control nurses, quality assurance nurses, case managers and nurses to fill out bed sore sheets every shift. All of this adds up and, of course, is paid for by the patients.

The hospitals are being squeezed by the insurance cartel. The federal government may pay an insurance company to manage an HMO (health maintenance organization) comprised of Medicaid patients, paying the HMO 113% of what is paid Medicare. The insurance company then gives the hospital 80% of what is given Medicare. The hospital may want to take a smaller amount from one of the HMOs to accommodate some of its staff doctors, but if the hospital does this, other HMOs will lower their payments and bankrupt the hospital.

One hospital bill of $25,258.18, the insurance company paid $5,759.79, the patient paid about $500 and $19,087.52 was written off. If the hapless patient had no insurance, or if the insurance company refuses to cover the hospitalization (pre-existing condition), the hospital wants the full amount. If the hospital bill exceeds a certain amount, the insurance company will pay more than the original discounted amount. It, therefore, is to the hospital's advantage to pad the bill as much as possible. If any other business took advantage of its customers the way that hospitals do, they probably would be put in jail.

There are several ways that the hospital can increase your bill:

- Charge you for things that you don't get.

- Charge you too much for the things that you do get.

- Leaving you in the recovery room or in the emergency room too long, waiting for housekeeping to clean your room.

- When your doctor discharges you at 11 AM and the hospital lets you out at 12 PM.

- Adding a "technical anesthesia charge" when you have already paid for the doctor, the room, the machines and the drugs.

- Leaving oxygen on patient after leaving the recovery room.

- Charging you to roll you to and from the operating room and charging you to wait in the holding area of the operating room.

Several years ago, an anesthesiologist wife had a baby at one of the large church hospitals. When he checked the bill, he noticed that his wife was charged for an epidural anesthesia and a pudendal block (the first, spinal and the second, local) as well as enough phenergan shots to sedate his wife until Whitsuntide. Perhaps the spinal anesthesia did not work and they had to resort to local anesthesia. However, when he brought this to the attention of the business office, he was told, "That's how we make money." This is the church fleecing you.

The EMTAIA Law demands that a hospital emergency room examine and stabilize all comers without inquiring as to his ability to pay. The patient cannot be transferred to another hospital unless the receiving hospital agrees to accept the patient. When Bubba falls off his motorcycle and sticks his broken tibia in the dirt and when his hospital bill is $100,000, the hospital, if on a 10% margin, will have to take in a million dollars to make up for Bubba.

Now comes the federal government's disproportionate share program to the rescue. If a hospital treats a disproportionate number of Medicare, Medicaid and non-resourse patients (free), then the federal government (taxpayers) gives the hospital money. One small hospital got 6-7 million dollars a year in dispro money, without which the hospital could not have survived. The EMTAIA (anti-dumping) law along with the disproportionate share program given us federal health care without calling it that. As with everything else, federal government equals in efficiency – free market (capitalism) equals efficiency.

The PCA pump (patient controlled administration) is a device that delivers a basal amount of intravenous narcotics to a patient continuously. When the patient hurts, he can press a button and get a dose of IV narcotic. Of course, the frequency that the patient can do this is controlled. This is a great deal for the hospital because a nurse doesn't have to draw up medicine and inject it into the patient. The patient not only is charged for the medicine but he is also charged for using the pump. The patient may be getting more narcotics than he needs and if he has had an abdominal operation, his intestinal motility may take longer to restart, necessitating another day in the hospital – bigger hospital bill. Rarely the pump or more likely the pumper malfunctions and kills the patient.

Hospitals are required to be inspected by the Joint Commission on Accrediting Hospitals and by Medicare. This is to keep the hospitals safe for patients. Much of what the Joint Commission on Accreditation of Hospitals requires is nitpicking and expensive – increasing hospital bills.

Nurses are supposed to periodically show the patient a sketch of ten faces – from smile to frown and ask the patient which one best describes his pain. The patient may not be having pain but he may get shot anyway. Some more expense dreamed up by the bureaucrats.

Hospitals have things written in Braille on the doors and on the elevators. Braille is written on the door to the doctor's dressing room in the surgery suite. Perhaps it is there for the housekeepers but I think that it is axiomatic that if one has to read Braille, he should not be operating on people. This is only a minor expense and who knows, maybe someday someone who reads Braille will need to get in the doctor's dressing room.

When being admitted to a hospital, one is required to fill out an advanced directive form, instructing ones caregivers to or not to administer measures to keep you alive if death is imminent. I would not sign one of these advanced directives, withholding care. After a big operation, one may be breathing all right but later may need to be put temporarily on a respirator because the anesthetic narcotic was still working, the pain and trauma of the surgery may depress ones breathing and the narcotics necessary for pain might depress ones respiration. A nurse who finished nursing school, God knows where, might read this advanced directive requesting no heroic measures and not call someone to put you on a respirator. Because no one dies at home any more, ones biggest medical expense is at the end of one's life. This advanced directive sounds like something that the insurance cartel cooked-up to help their bottom line.

As a result of not signing this advanced directive asking that no extreme measures be used to keep you alive, one cannot peacefully die at the end of one's life. The crash cart will be hauled out and people will start pumping on your chest trying to resurrect you. The excuse is that we might get sued if we don't try to resurrect this patient. Trying to resurrect someone is not cheap. One has two choices. One can sign for no heroic measures and run the risk of needlessly dying or of having the team futilely trying to resurrect you by pounding on your chest after you were dead.

Investor owned hospitals are not on equal footing with non-profit (church owned) hospitals. Investor owned hospitals pay taxes, non-profit hospitals don't. The two compete but the non-profit hospitals are allowed to advertise.

St. Joseph's Hospital, which subsequently has been sold to a private company, had an inadequate number of useable laparoscopes but had a large Sister's of Commerce fountain on a corner where land was worth several hundred dollars a square foot. The Fountain appeared to be a big pile of rocks with water cascading down. It reminded one of Splash Mountain at Disney World. These non-profit hospitals, paying no taxes, can do whatever they please. That is, until they go broke.

Patient No: 00000   Billing Date: 08/13/05

Ied Rec No: 0000   Admitted: 02/23/05

Guarantor No: Discharged: 02/27/05

Patient: XXXXXXXX

Departmental Charge Summary

Dept	Description	Amount
0610	Med Surg	3,633.00
0701	Operating Room	6,226.32
0704	Pacu	1,472.60
0712	Pharmacy	1,752.70
0715	I.V. Therapy	2,570.40
0718	Central Supply	1,773.26
0722	Anesthesia	2,377.82
0728	Radiology	297.24
0736	Lab	3,168.82
0754	Resp. Therapy	994.30
0758	Blood Bank	576.00
0763	Nuclear Med	207.86
0780	Treatment Room	207.86

Total Charges:	25,258.18
Total Payments:	5,759.79
Total Adjust:	19,087.52

Patient No: 00000   Billing Date: 08/13/05

Ied Rec No: 0000   Admitted: 02/23/05

Guarantor No: Discharged: 02/27/05

Patient: XXXXXXXX

Date of Payment	Batch Refer	Pay Type	Proc	Ins Plan	Bill thru DT	Description/ Comment	Amount
02/23/05	24W831	1	014950			WM1101T Pmt Check	401.25
02/27/05	02FBIL	5	999999	313-04	02/27/05	Contractual Adj	19,367.88
03/11/05	11BC67	1	015435	313-04	02/27/05	Era BC P 03/09/05	5,358.54
03/11/05	11LREV	5	999999	313-04	02/27/05	Contractual Adj	19,367.88-
03/11/05	11RMIT	5	999999	313-04	02/27/05	Contractual Adj	19,087.52
						Total Payments	24,847.31

Total Charges	25258.18
Payments	5759.79
Adjustments	19087.52
Balance	410.87

Patient No: 00000
Ied Rec No: 0000
Guarantor No:
Patient: XXXXXXXXX

Billing Date: 08/13/05
Admitted: 02/23/05
Discharged: 02/27/05

Date of Service	Batch Refer	Dept	Proc	NDC/ CPT-4/ HCPCS	Qty	Service Description	Charges
				272-Sterile Supplies			
022305	23B431	0718	034155		1	Cathlon IV 20 Ga 1-1/4	26.43
022305	23B431	0718	032818		1	Set I.V. 2C5527	46.62
022305	23B431	0718	014525		1	Blood-Y Set	83.85
022305	24B536	0718	014525		1	Blood-Y Set	83.85
022405	25B666	0718	012232		1	Bovie Ground Pad	37.06
022405	25B666	0718	012233		1	Bovie Pencil	37.06
022405	25B666	0718	027638		1	Foley Cath Tray w/bg	101.01
022405	25B666	0718	036312		1	Smoke Evacuator Filter	93.24
022405	25B666	0718	036376		1	Smoke Evacuator Tubing	142.14
022405	25B666	0718	049352		1	Sponge Radiopaque 4 X	15.53
022405	25B666	0718	049353		2	Sponge Lap Pk/5	98.42
022405	25B666	0718	500220		2	Pds 1 CTX Z371T	62.14
022405	25B666	0718	500843	#1	3	Vicryl 0 CT1 J740D	324.42
022405	25B666	0718	500856		2	Vicryl 20 CT1 J345H	53.42
022405	25B666	0718	500878		1	Plain 20 CT1 843H	25.07
022405	25B666	0718	012333		1	Tubing PCA	49.05
022405	25B666	0718	017584		1	Cath Suc Control14FR	12.26
022405	25B666	0718	017586		1	Cath Secure	22.89
022405	25B666	0718	019001		1	Circuit Anes	82.57
022405	25B666	0718	026135		1	Endo Tube 7.0	52.78
022405	25B666	0718	032818		1	Set I.V. 2C5527	46.62
022405	25B666	0718	033945		1	IV Set Secondary 2C745	22.33
022405	25B666	0718	034153		1	Cathlon IV 18GA X 1-3/	26.43
022405	25B666	0718	046842		1	Salem Sump Tube	46.30
						Subtotal:	1591.49
				301-Chemistry			
022305	23B429	0736	847010	84702	1	HCG Beta Quantitative	245.96
022305	23B429	0736	830200	83020	1	Hemoglobin Electro	64.76
022405	24B468	0736	800070	80053 #2	1	Comp Metabolic Panel	347.46
						Subtotal:	658.18
				302- Immunology			
022305	23B429+	0736	860800	86900	4	ABO Type	315.92
022305	23B429	0736	861000	86901	1	RH Type	67.21
022305	23B429	0736	860230	86850	1	Antibody Screen Ea	145.49
022305	23B429	0736	860740	86920	3	Crossmatch Imm Spin	580.86
022305	23B521	0736	860740	86920	2	Crossmatch Imm Spin	387.24
022305	23B521	0736	860800	86900	2	ABO Type	157.96
						Subtotal:	1654.68

Patient No: 00000
Ied Rec No: 0000
Guarantor No:
Patient: XXXXXXXX

Billing Date: 08/13/05
Admitted: 02/23/05
Discharged: 02/27/05

Date of Service	Batch Refer	Dept	Proc	NDC/ CPT-4/ HCPCS	Qty	Service Description	Charges
				305-Hematology			
022305	23B429	0736	850280	85025	1	CBC Platelet Auto Diff	126.09
022305	23B429	0736	856100	85610	1	Protime	103.92
022305	23B429	0736	857300	85730	1	PTT	121.59
022405	24B468+	0736	850280	85025	2	CBC Platelet Auto Diff	252.18
022505	25B571	0736	850280	85025	1	CBC Platelet Auto Diff	126.09
022605	25B571	0736	850280	85025	1	CBC Platelet Auto Diff	126.09
						Subtotal:	855.96
				324-X-Ray Chest			
022305	23B435	0728	710203	71020	1	XR Chest 2 V	297.24
						Subtotal:	297.24
				360-OR Service			
022405	25B666	0701	500254		1	OR Initial 30 Minutes	1779.37
022405	25B666	0701	500675		5	OR Each Add 30 Min	3708.65
						Subtotal:	5488.02
				370-Anesthesia Svs			
022405	25B666	0722	500970		1	Anes Int 30 Min	872.62
022405	25B666	0722	50997		5	Anes Each Add 30 Min	1505.20
						Subtotal:	2377.82
				390-Blood Storage General			
022305	23B429+	0758	895020	P9016	2	PRBC LR	384.00
022305	23B465	0758	895020	P9016	1	PRBC LR	192.00
						Subtotal:	576.00
				410-Respiratory Svc			
022405	25B652	0754	978319	94640	1	Inh TX AC Awy Obst	169.71
						Subtotal:	169.71
				460-Pulmonary Function			
022505	25B652	0754	948319	94760	1	Noninv Ear OR Puls OX	45.04
						Subtotal:	45.04
				710-Recovery			
022405	25B666	0704	992693		1	Rec Room Initial 30 Mi	741.34
022405	25B666	0704	992694		4	Rec Room Addtl 30 Min	593.04
						Subtotal:	1334.38
				730-EKG/ECG			
022305	25B433	0763	714152	93005	1	EKG Tracing Only	207.86
022305	23B415	0780	930004	93005	1	EKG Tracing Only	207.86
						Subtotal:	415.72
						Total Ancillary Charges	21625.18

Patient No: 00000
Ied Rec No: 0000
Guarantor No:
Patient: XXXXXXXX

Billing Date: 08/13/05
Admitted: 02/23/05
Discharged: 02/27/05

Date of Service	Batch Refer	Dept	Proc	NDC/CPT-4/HCPCS	Qty	Service Description	Charges
022605	26B729	0712	712426	51079093320	1	Hydrocod/Apap 5/500	3.56
022705	27B758	0712	712522	6096328	1	Pepcid 20Mg Tablet	13.92
022705	27B758	0712	712426	51079093320	1	Hydrocod/Apap 5/500	3.56
						Subtotal:	88.43
				258-IV Solutions			
022305	23B434+	0715	202981	264180000	2	Normal Sal 1000 CC	257.04
022405	24B523+	0715	201340	264175100	14	D5LR 1000ML	1799.28
022505	24B573+	0715	201340	264175100	3	D5LR 1000ML	385.56
022605	24B524	0715	201340	264175100	1	D5LR 1000ML	128.52
						Subtotal:	2570.40
				259-Pharmacy Other			
022305	23B434	0712	139142	182844700	29	Acetaminoph 325MG TB	9.28
022605	26B691+	0712	113500	51079001920	3	Docusate 100MG Cap	2.10
022605	26B691	0712	125555	615062513	2	Simethicone 80MG Tab	.70
022705	27B758	0712	113500	51079001920	1	Docusate 100MG Cap	.70
						Subtotal:	12.78
				270-Med-Surg Supplies			
022305	23B431	0718	034203		1	IV J-Loop	15.53
022305	23B431	0718	033710		1	IV Injection Site	22.33
022405	25B572	0754	950300		7	RT-Oxygen Therapy Add	363.79
022405	25B666	0718	014195		1	Benzoin	15.53
022405	25B666	0718	024377		1	Elbow/Heel Protector	62.82
022405	25B666	0701	049014		1	Compression Sleeve Med	273.25
022405	25B666	0718	049468		2	Sponge Gauze 4X4	21.26
022405	25B666	0718	053708		1	Telfa Dressing 3X8	11.45
022405	25B666	0718	019197		1	Clear Wound Dr 2X3	24.60
022405	25B666	0718	034203		1	IV J-Loop	15.53
022405	25B666	0718	044780		1	Probe Esop Temp	88.06
022405	25B666	0718	044870		1	Probe Pulse Oximeter	103.92
022405	25B666	0718	051294		1	Stylet Adult	31.61
022405	25B666	0718	060486		1	Yankauer Suction Tip	24.29
022405	25B666	0704	963152		1	Rec RM 02	138.22
022505	25B652	0754	950300		8	RT-Oxygen Therapy Add	415.76
						Subtotal:	1627.95
				271-Non-Sterile-Supply			
022405	25B666	0718	012201		1	ABD Binder	11.45
022405	25B666	0718	012211		1	Airway Oral Adult	24.60
022505	25B640	0718	012203		1	Abominal Binder 12”	173.84
						Subtotal:	209.89

Patient No: 00000
Ied Rec No: 0000
Guarantor No:
Patient: XXXXXXXX

Billing Date: 08/13/05
Admitted: 02/23/05
Discharged: 02/27/05

Date of Service	Att Phys	FC	Room	AC	Serv Code	Rev Code	Dept	Room and Care	Charges
02/23/05	5884	13	210A	P	GSUR	111	0610	4 Days at 908.25	3,633.00
								Total Room and Care	3,633.00

Date of Service	Batch Refer	Dept	Proc	NDC/CPT-4/HCPCS	Qty	Service Description	Charges
				250-Pharmacy			
022305	01B911	0712	133267	60977015503	1	Robinul 1MG/5CC	32.06
022305	01B911	0712	122131	186024213	1	Lido 2% 5 ML SDV PF	28.07
022305	01B911	0712	126881	703270403	1	Neostigmine 10CC	63.06
022305	01B911	0712	712221	173044202	1	Zofran 4MG/2ML Inj	152.82
022305	01B911	0712	113260	310029020	1	Diprivan 20ML Amp	97.70
022305	01B911	0712	133442	52045015	2	Rocuronium 50MG Inj	257.06
022305	01B911	0712	712243	74445602	1	Ultane 250ML	474.96
022405	24B539	0712	712170	4692306	2	Ketorolac 30 MG Inj	124.96
022405	24B558	0712	135412	11098003005	1	Sublimaze 5ML	47.27
022405	24B558	0712	140085	4199806	1	Versed 2MG Inj	43.06
022405	24B523	0712	712184	24126308	1	MS 10MG Syring	37.07
022405	24B523	0712	124940	338268975	1	Morphine Syringe/PCA	142.72
022405	24B500	0712	102645	7313705	1	Cefazol 1GM/ D5W 50ML	150.68
						Subtotal:	1651.49
				251-Generic Drugs			
022305	23B434	0712	712386	57480032101	1	Diphenhyd 25MG Cap	.70
022405	24B500	0712	712475	51079028320	1	Metoclopram 10MG Tab	11.01
022405	24B500	0712	712522	6096328	1	Pepcid 20MG Tablet	13.92
022405	24B500	0712	712522	6096328	1	Pepcid 20MG Tablet	13.92
022405	24B500	0712	712522	6096328	2	Pepcid 20MG Tablet	27.84
022405	24B500	0712	712522	6096328	1	Pepcid 20MG Tablet	13.92-
022405	24B500	0712	712522	6096328	1	Pepcid 20MG Tablet	13.92

FDA

It is alleged that it cost 1.4 billion dollars to bring a new drug to market – phase one study, phase two study, phase three study, etc. The FDA doesn't want any more drugs, that caused babies to be born without limbs as did thalidomide, nor Vioxx that supposedly increased the incidence of heart attacks, but it takes too much time and money to bring a drug to market. Some foreign pharmaceutical companies market their new drugs outside the U.S. because of the cost of testing required by the FDA.

A drug used to sclerosis varicose veins was used successfully in Europe for 10-20 years but would not be approved by the FDA. The drug was superior to the drug used in the U.S. because it was less likely to turn brown the overlying skin. One doctor's license was suspended for using it. The FDA procrastinated so long that both drugs were made obsolete by laser technology. Politics, anyone?

Small pharmaceutical companies, trying to develop a new drug, have a "crash and burn" date when they run out of money (capital) – bankruptcy follows.

The FDA did not approve the cancer drug, Erbitux. Martha Stewart and Pete, her stockbroker, were sent to "Club Fed" (federal minimum security prison) for a short stint because Martha was told by Pete that there was a rumor on the floor that Sam, the company president, was selling his stock. Because Martha and Pete had previously talked about selling the stock at 60 anyway, this would be a good time to sell. Martha and Sam were friends but she was not charged with insider trading – she was charged with lying! The court alleged that Martha and Pete did not talk about selling the stock at 60, even though there is no way of knowing what Martha and Pete talked about. The jury was not allowed to be told that Martha and Pete were not charged with insider trading. What if Martha and Pete said, "We sold the stock because we heard that Sam was selling his?" And the court said, "No, you didn't, you sold your stock because a black cat ran across the road in front of your car when you were coming to work that morning." You are lying, you are going to jail. This case sounds worse than Russia.

The stock of Martha Stewarts company opened up the morning that Judge Cedarbaum gave Martha and Pete a much lighter than expected sentence.

After Martha and Pete went off to the slammer, the FDA decided that they would approve the cancer drug, Erbitux. The company's stock rebounded.

If the FDA takes too long to approve a drug developed by a small pharmaceutical company, then a large pharmaceutical company can take them over much cheaper in the bankruptcy court than when the small pharmaceutical company is solvent. Politics anyone?

Perhaps the FDA is paralyzed worrying about releasing a drug such as Vioxx that will generate class-action law suits and bankruptcy of a large pharmaceutical company.

Many millions were awarded to victims of silicone breast implants. The silicone implants were recalled by the FDA. Now, the implants have been approved for limited use.

The FDA is neither serving well the populace nor the pharmaceutical industry. There must be some limitation of liability for a pharmaceutical company that spends 1.4 billion dollars developing and testing a drug that later is found to have a previously unknown side effect.

The onerous burden placed on the pharmaceutical companies by the FDA not only increases the cost of medicines but also allows people to die or go blind waiting for a drug to be approved for use.

The 1.4 billion dollars necessary to bring a drug to market, in a large part is caused by the expense of clinical trails-phase 1,phase 11,phase 111. Many of the FDA doctors probably came from institutions that do medical and drug research, and they probably plan to return to these institutions after their government service. Many drugs are not accepted for review the first time that they are submitted to the FDA. More studies are required, which means that more revenue is generated for the research institutions, from where some of the FDA doctors came and to where the FDA doctors plan to return. Some might consider that some of the FDA doctors might have a conflict of interest.

More studies mean that some of the small pharmaceutical companies might run out of money and go bankrupt, which allows the large pharmaceutical companies to buy the small pharmaceutical companies with their developing drug,undeveloped drug or unaccepted drugs at a bankruptcy sale. Do the FDA doctors then get to develop those drugs for large pharmaceutical companies at the FDA doctors 'institutions? If this is the case than no wonder our drugs cost so much. It is not good to have a system based on the honesty, the integrity, and the altruism of doctors and the corporate executives.

Lawyers

It has been estimated that litigation, fear of litigation, and defensive medicine, which now has morphed into maximizing income by hospitals, doctors, and ambulance companies' accounts for one third of the health care cost.

Mr. Shakespeare wanted to kill all of the lawyers, but the lawyers are but pawns the insurance cartel. The insurance cartel pays lawyers exorbitant fees to defend unmeritorious medical malpractice suits, resulting in exorbitant medical malpractice premiums. Hospital liability premiums follow. As a result, health insurance premiums increase as do Workman's Compensation premiums. Throw in defensive medicine costs and the cost of maximizing income by hospitals and doctors under the guise of defensive medicine and then the corporations, strapped with this onerous health care burden have become uncompetitive on world markets.

One cannot have a meaningful lawsuit without a rich defendant or an insured defendant. There aren't many rich defendants. Therefore, the insurance cartel is at the center of the problem.

A plastic surgeon was sued for damaging a patient's spinal accessory nerve while doing liposuction in the patient's neck, causing the patient to have a "winged-scapula", i.e. the shoulder blade sticks out from the body. The spinal accessory nerve comes from the brain and is just beneath the skin in the lateral part of the neck on its way to the muscles of the scapula (shoulder blade). It takes little trauma to cause this nerve not to function for a few months.

The anesthesiologist was also named in the suit for allegedly holding the patients head crooked during the procedure. The anesthesiologist was dropped from the suit without ever being deposed or going to court. His insurance carrier wrote him a letter telling him that they had spent $90,000 defending him. At $300 an hour, that is working twenty-four hours a day for almost two weeks. Why would an insurance company pay a lawyer this much money for so little work that was needed? Perhaps the insurance adjuster and the lawyer were cousins or were real good friends. Most likely, the insurance company wanted it so that it could increase everybody's premiums, thus giving the insurance company more money to invest in bonds, real estate and politicians. The plastic surgeon won the suit. No doubt the patient's nerve had recovered by the time of the trial.

When I started practicing surgery in Houston, my malpractice insurance premiums were $600 a year. By the time I quit practicing surgery the annual premiums were close to $50,000. All inflations end when people can no longer afford that which is being inflated. We have reached that point with malpractice insurance. Hospitals require doctors to have malpractice insurance to work in the hospital. Many doctors bought only the minimum coverage required by the hospital – an amount that did not protect the doctor. The insurance cartel further strapped the doctors by selling only claims made policies. Occurrence policies cover the doctor when the malpractice occurred. Claims made policies cover the doctor when the suit is filed or perhaps when the doctor is notified that a suit will be filed. Most malpractice suits usually aren't filed until a year after the occurrence; therefore, if the doctor had a real bad lawsuit, the insurance company could not renew the "good-doctors" insurance. The malpractice premiums now are but a tribute paid to the insurance cartel for allowing the doctor to practice medicine.

For one small hospital, the premiums for the first million dollars insurance was $900,000. The hospital had to self–insure the first million dollars. Guess who pays for this – the patients.

The only infectious disease specialist at one hospital refuses to see pediatric patients because the statute of limitations run until the patient is twenty-one years old. Surgeons use this as an excuse not to operate on pediatric patients with appendicitis! No matter what time the patient comes to the hospital, it seems that most appendectomies are done at night. It is not worth $300-$400, if the doctor can collect it, for the surgeon to stay up half the night.

O.J. Simpson was found innocent of murdering his wife and Mr. Goldman. Although criminal defense lawyers all have the same fee – everything you got. O.J. still had some assets, therefore he was sued in the civil court. Why isn't this double jeopardy? Had O.J. any money left, the federal court could have charged him with violating the civil rights of the victims, as the government does in Mississippi and Alabama when a jury does not convict rednecks for killing black people. It would then be triple jeopardy. O.J. must have accumulated a little money. From looking at his golf swing on TV, I doubt that he won it playing golf. Now the lawyers are after him again in Las Vegas.

The Texas Rio Grande Valley is one of the most litigious areas of the country. A general surgeon in Brownsville was paying $60,000 in malpractice insurance premiums. At one time, there was only one neurosurgeon in the Rio Grande Valley. Consequently, head injury patients died without ever being seen by a neurosurgeon.

A tank truck skidded off the road in the valley and killed and injured a number of people at a Fiesta or Quinceañera (Mexican Bat Mitzvah). A ten million dollar judgment was rendered against the company that made the tank that was part of the rig ten years ago. The company that made the tank was one of the best tank makers in the country. The company's insurance premiums went from two thousand dollars a year to $600,000 a year. The owner closed the plant, laid off 300 people, had a heart attack and died. Not a nation of laws, but a nation of lawyers.

I was told by a retired ophthalmologist from northern Mississippi that he wanted to work part time but he could not afford the malpractice insurance. There was a county seat in northern Mississippi that had more lawsuits filed than there were people living in the county seat. Apparently, a person would get a Phen-fen prescription in California and get it filled in Mississippi, take two pills and file a lawsuit alleging that Phen-fen caused heart failure. In one case at trial, in spite of expert testimony stating that the plaintiff did not have heart failure, the jury awarded the plaintiff six million dollars because he feared that he might get heart failure. One juror wanted the plaintiff to give him a tip for being so generous. It's no wonder that health care costs so much.

A pathologist diagnosed a woman as having breast cancer and the surgeon removed her breast. The patient's brother, a pathologist in an adjacent city reviewed the slides and said that his sister did not have breast cancer. All of his colleagues agreed. All of the original pathologist's colleagues said that it was a cancer. The patient sued the pathologist and won a three million dollar judgment. The pathologist had one million dollars insurance. The pathologist had a heart attack and died while looking at his bank statement.

As a result of this case, many doctors quit doing frozen sections on breast lumps, resulting in two operations if the patient had a breast cancer. Breast biopsy slides were sent to the MD Anderson Cancer Hospital for review until the hospital became overwhelmed and quit reviewing the slides. Now, stereotactic needle biopsy has helped solve the problem.

In Texas, a constitutional amendment was passed limiting damages for pain and suffering in medical malpractice suits to $250,000. Economic damages were unchanged. Four to six weeks before the amendment came into effect, three thousand medical malpractice suits were filed in Harris County (Houston) Texas where eight to nine thousand doctors practice. That is about a third of the doctors in the county getting sued in 1-2 months. My, we had a lot of bad doctors that month.

Mr. Scruggs, the Mississippi billionaire tobacco class action lawyer, was carping the plaintiff's lawyer's party line that the malpractice crisis was caused by a few bad doctors and that all that we had to do to solve the problem was to get rid of these bad apples. Several years ago, I looked up Dr. Denton Cooley and Dr. Michael DeBakey's lawsuits at the courthouse. Dr. Cooley had seventy (some other than malpractice) and Dr. DeBakey had ten. Dr. Cooley was the best heart surgeon in the world, Dr. DeBakey was the premier surgeon in the world and was summoned to Russia to preside over Premier Yeltsin's heart operation.

In Dr. DeBakey's (then in his 90s) recent case, his dentist sued him because the dentist allegedly was impotent after an abdominal aneurysm operation that Dr. DeBakey advised him to have. Dr. DeBakey did not operate on him, nor did he have him sign a consent sheet. After our pissant lawyers and judges dragged the premier surgeon in the world through the court for two weeks, Dr. DeBakey prevailed when his lawyer extolled the virtues of Viagra.

Florida was considering revoking the license of any doctor who had three malpractice judgments against him. Florida must have a short memory. It wasn't long ago that no neurosurgeon would come to an ER in Miami. If this law is enacted:
1. Doctors won't come to Florida.
2. Doctors will leave Florida.
3. Lawyers will extort money from doctors by filing and making doctors settle suits.
4. Doctors won't treat high risk (sick) patients.

In Florida, a bedsore could be a criminal offense – mistreating old people. Patients with low serum albumen (proteins in the blood) tend to get bed sores. Nursing homes and hospitals may turn away patients with low serum albumen.

Recently, the phrase mongers and propagandist of the media were lamenting the decrease in the uses of mammography – predicting an increase in the deaths from breast cancer. Reading mammograms is a large generator of malpractice lawsuits, consequently, some doctors, hospitals and clinics quit doing mammograms, resulting in more costs for the health care system.

Medicaid mom brings child to Emergency Room because child has a knot on his head where he bumped it. Although the chances of a fractured skull is very small and home observation would not be bad treatment, if there were a small fracture and the patient was not knocked unconscious. An x-ray is done. The ER doctor does not want to be charged with missing a skull fracture and be set upon by Medicaid, the crusading TV personality, a pack of plaintiff lawyers and have the Texas State Board of Medical Examiners launch an investigation that would take longer than O.J.'s trial.

The same principle applies to CAT scans in the ER for patients with abdominal pain. Sending a patient with appendicitis out of the ER is another leading cause of medical malpractice suits. A patient may have obvious appendicitis and need an operation regardless of what a Cat scan shows but he gets a CT anyway. A child may have abdominal pain but no vomiting and minimal tenderness and a normal white blood count. He could go home and return in the early morning or sooner if his condition changes, but a Cat scan is done. The child may develop appendicitis five days from now and go to another hospital. The first hospital would be incriminated.

An ICU nurse gets sudden lower abdominal pain in the middle of her menstrual cycle. Although she probably had a ruptured ovarian follicle, a Cat scan was done. The ER bill was $3,000, not counting the radiologist bill – she had no insurance – defensive medicine at its best. There was a minor auto accident and one of the victims was walking around at the scene when the ambulance arrived. She said that her shoulder hurt and that her neck hurt a little. When one of probably several ambulances arrived, a plastic collar was placed around her neck and her head and her body were taped to the board on which she was placed. When the patient arrived at an emergency room, a cross-table lateral x-ray of the neck was done before removing the neck collar and before removing the tape holding her to the board, in case her neck was broken. Other x-rays were then done – all normal, of course. No one wants to get sued for missing a broken neck – besides, the lawyers need the x-rays.

I was defended in an unmeritorious (nuisance) lawsuit by a law firm that was capitated by the insurance company. Capitated means that the insurance company gives the law firm a certain amount of money per doctor, that the insurance company insures, whether the doctor is sued or not. In this case, a summary judgment was obtained in a New York minute.

Had the lawyers not been capitated, there probably would have been dispositions that took up the better part of a day with five or six lawyers making $300 an hour asking inane questions and taking many "breaks".

When I was a third string high school football player – probably fourth string if they had one, I tried to tackle a big old boy with legs like tree stumps as he ran through a hole in the line. I woke up over on the grass with no one around me. The scrimmage was still going on. I got up and walked up to the coach, who chewed me out for getting hurt. I went home and ate supper.

Today, an ambulance would come, put a collar around my neck, tape me to a board, and haul me off to an emergency room where x-rays and a Cat scan would be done. The difference between then and today is that today I would have a multi-thousand dollar hospital bill and I would be late for supper.

By mistake, I received a campaign flyer from a judge running for higher office. The flyer said that I cannot accept more than $30,000 from one law firm – probably unsaid was no less either. Who would you like to represent you? A lawyer whose firm gave the judge $30,000 or a lawyer whose firm didn't? In Texas, one is entitled to all of the justice that one can afford.

Houston must have been the epicenter of the silicone breast implant lawsuits. The local doctor would also be named in the lawsuit to keep Dow-Corning from removing the suit to a federal court because of diversity, where a federal judge would be less likely to go along with this alleged thievery. When the breast implant was removed and was found to have leaked, the patient received money – if it didn't leak, she didn't receive money. Ergo, it was incumbent on the plaintiff lawyer to get a very observant plastic surgeon to remove the implants. After millions or billions of dollars in awards the government said that it was all right to use the implants again in some cases.

A newspaper article by Mary Flood in the Houston Chronicle cited a case where RGM Construction sued Tribble & Stephens for a $12,000 unpaid debt. RGM lost on appeal and a jury was to decide how much RGM must pay Tribble & Stephens' attorneys. The case had been litigated for nine years and Tribble & Stephens' attorneys wanted 1.5 million dollars. The jury awarded them $50,000. RGM had paid their attorneys $500,000. If insurance companies were paying these lawyers, then everyone's rates will go up as in medical malpractice suits. Let us say it again. "We are not a nation of laws but are a nation of lawyers" – to the detriment of all.

The feds closed a small bank in a small town near Houston and sent the president and majority stock owner to Club Fed (federal minimum security prison) for a few months. The feds sold the bank to a large Houston bank for $225,000, even though the bank president had been offered seven million dollars for the bank. Obviously, the large Houston bank had political connections with the party in power.

The feds also sued the bank board. The board members never saw U.S. attorneys but instead they dealt with private attorneys that were allegedly paid three million dollars to handle the case. If a U.S. attorney can dole out three million dollars of business to his friends, or perhaps future law partners, then he might find victims to prosecute whether they need prosecuting or not.

If three million tax dollars was spent on a $225,000 bank, then how much money, if any, was spent on private attorneys persecuting Martha Stewart, who violated no laws?

EMTALA

The EMTALA Law (Emergency Medical Treatment and Active Labor Act), dubbed the "Anti-dumping Law" by the phrase-mongers and propagandists probably has increased the cost of health care more than any other malcontrivance generated by our lawmakers. The EMTALA Law dictates that anyone who comes to a hospital emergency room must be examined and stabilized and that the patient cannot be transferred to another hospital (e.g. charity patient to a charity hospital) unless the receiving hospital and receiving doctor agree to accept the patient. An EMTALA violation carries a $50,000 fine and possibly a loss of being able to treat Medicare and Medicaid patients – in other words, out of business for many hospitals. The law further states that the receiving hospital must accept the patient if the receiving hospital can provide a needed higher level of care unavailable at the sending hospital – if the receiving hospital has the beds. The receiving hospital doesn't want the patient because they are overwhelmed taking care of illegal aliens that use up to 30% of their budget. When a patient arrives at an ER, he cannot be asked about his insurance or about his ability to pay.

The EMTALA Law probably was passed to give us socialized medicine – universal coverage without universal payment. The hospitals and the doctors are held in involuntary servitude, however, the hospitals are reimbursed through the disproportionate share program, a government program that gives money to hospitals that treat a disproportionate number of Medicare, Medicaid and non-resource patients.

The doctors work for free. I was told that initially the disproportionate money was to also go to the doctors, but the doctors did not know about the dispro program for several years after it started. What is wrong with the doctors doing a little charity work? It seems that all of these patients are at night, even if the patient came to the ER during the day and these are the patients most likely to sue. Because of lack of resources, these patients wait too long to seek medical attention, thus they are sicker and more likely to have a bad outcome. As a condition to being on a hospital staff, doctors are required to take emergency room call – the doctors can either be held in involuntary servitude or not work.

The EMTALA Law has turned out emergency rooms into twenty-four hour out-patient dispensaries. The hospitals don't mind because they are paid fifteen-twenty times what a doctor is paid for seeing the patient in his office.

Because the hospital does not want to be fined and because the hospital makes money, flagrant abuse by patients is allowed.

Some large hospitals now have "fast track" at the hospital or off-site satellite "emergency rooms" that don't take patients brought by ambulance. A few years ago there were twenty-four hour out-patient clinics, i.e. Doc-in-the-Box. Now we have the same thing but now because of the EMTALA Law (Emergency Medical Treatment and Active Labor Act) they are called satellite emergency rooms and about $180 is added to the bill as an ER charge. This extra charge is paid by insurance companies, Medicare and Medicaid – in other words, by we the people.

Our "Anti-dumping Law" now has morphed into a "Dumping Law." In Houston, when the two city/county (charity) hospitals say that their hospitals are full, they declare themselves on "Drive-by" status. In other words, ambulances take their patients to private hospitals, which are then stuck with the expense of taking care of the city/county's non-resource patients.

A man has a urethral discharge for two weeks and comes to the ER at 1:30 AM by ambulance.

A patient had sutures put in twenty days ago at the city/county hospital and she comes to the ER at 2 AM to have them removed.

A patient comes to the ER by ambulance (red or white taxi), is treated and sent home. The ER doctor forgot to put his narcotics number on her prescription, therefore she calls the ambulance again to return her to the ER again to have the ER doctor put his narcotic number on her prescription. The pharmacist could have called.

A child has had a runny nose and fever for two days. The child is brought to the ER or Fast Track at midnight because there is a short wait or is brought to the ER at 5:30 AM before Dad goes to work. The pediatrician's office opens at nine AM.

A patient with a subdural hematoma (blood clot around the brain) came to the ER in a small hospital about forty miles from Houston. The patient urgently needed a neurosurgeon to put holes in the patient's skull to remove the blood clot. Because of the EMTALA Law, it was necessary to call nine hospitals before a hospital in Lufkin, Texas agreed to accept the patient. This patient needed "dumping" to a place that could take care of her.

A patient comes to an emergency room and asked to see her doctor. She was told that her doctor was not on the hospital staff and that she should call him. When the patient said that she did not have fifty cents for the pay phone, the nurse dialed the phone and handed it to the patient. Wham, an EMTALA violation. The patient should have been examined and stabilized, or better still, let the patient dial the phone. The hospital CEO said that he would be glad to pay a $50,000 fine because now the government was going to send an inspector. If the hospital did not like what the inspector said, the hospital could mobilize its big time lawyers in Dallas and go to the Federal Court.

A patient comes to an ER in a small hospital four times in one month complaining of chest pain. Each time he tests positive for alcohol and cocaine. Each time, ECG, chest x-ray and lab are normal. He is observed. He has no resources and each time he refuses to go to the city/county hospital for a definitive work-up.

When a patient is transferred from one ER to another, the ER doctor has to sign his name three times on papers filled out by the nurse.

Except to give us socialized (government) medicine, why would our lawmakers pass such a wasteful law?

Our Senate is run by committees. The committees are run by seniority. In other words, our Senate is run by a bunch of old men. Some might surmise that the subtleties of senility have set in on some of our senior Senators.

Perhaps the Senators who passed the EMTALA Law are some of the same Senators who conducted the hearing when Judge Clarence Thomas was nominated to the Supreme Court. When I heard that Judge Thomas had taken a young lady to Tulsa for the weekend, I thought, that doesn't sound too good. But I thought that if Mrs. Thomas did not mind, why should the Senate? I kept listening and found out that the Judge was not married at the time and that the trip was eight years ago. When they started talking about hisself, the judge's penis, I thought, man, they ought to lock these old fools up.

Justice Rhenquest, terminally ill with thyroid cancer was the deciding vote to expand the eminent domain law to allow politicians to confiscate private property to allow their buddies to develop it. Should impaired leaders be allowed to make such important decisions? Perhaps when a Supreme Court Justice can no longer walk up the front steps to work, he should retire.

Texas Board

The charge of the Texas Board of Medical Examiners is to license and regulate the practice of medicine in the State of Texas.

The Board, however, has degenerated into lap dogs of the trial lawyers.

Adolph Hitler, or was it Mr. Geobble, said that if one tells the "Big Lie" often enough, people believe it. The malpractice crisis is caused by a few bad doctors and the way to remedy it is to get rid of these bad doctors.

The Texas State Board of Medical Examiners requires that if one is to practice medicine in the State of Texas, he must post in his office the address of the Board and State so that anyone can complain about his doctor by calling or writing them. This alone increases the number of malpractice suits.

When the Board receives a complaint, whether from an unhappy patient, one of the doctor's competitors or detractors, or a litigant at the behest of his lawyer, the Board writes the doctor, who they now refer to as the Licensee, asking him to respond to this complaint, violating his constitutional right against self-incrimination – the fifth amendment. The Board then notifies all of the hospitals in the state that the Board is investigating this doctor.

The Board will not tell the doctor who filed the complaint, because the Board says that this is only an investigation and not punishment. Every year when the doctor has to reapply for malpractice insurance, the doctor is asked, "Are you being investigated or have you ever been investigated by the Texas State Board of Medical Examiners?"

Most of the medical malpractice insurance written today is "claims made" and not occurrence insurance. Occurrence insurance means that one is covered for any maloccurence that occurred during the year that the maloccurence occurred. Claims made insurance means that one is covered for any claim made during the year that the claim is made. Well, guess what. The Statute of Limitations is two years or two years and forty-five days for other parties added to the suit. It usually takes more than one year for a suit to be filed. Therefore, if the insurance company hears of the complaint to the Texas Board of Medical Examiners, the insurance company will not renew the doctor's insurance. With claims made insurance, the doctor is not buying insurance but is paying tribute to the insurance cartel. If this isn't punishment by the Board, then what is?

All police states were started for a good reason – ours, to stamp out dope dealers, terrorists and bad doctors – and, not to mention, Martha Stewart.

The Texas Board of Medical Examiners wrote a "Licensee" that he had abandoned a patient. The Board did not bother to say that this infraction took place over ten years ago. What happened was that the doctor removed the patient's colon cancer and placed a venous access port over ten years ago. Over three thousand lawsuits were filed in Harris County (Houston) the 1-2 months before a constitutional amendment limiting damages for pain and suffering went in to effect. The patient had answered a newspaper ad of a lawyer who told her to file a complaint against the doctor with the Texas Board of Medical Examiners. Except for murder, military desertion, student infractions, and perhaps other heinous crimes, not many statutes run more than ten years.

A venous port is a small plastic or metal chamber with a plastic top that is put just beneath the skin, allowing medicine to be put in the chamber by sticking a needle through the skin. Attached to the chamber is a small plastic tube that has been put in a large vein in the chest by threading the tube over a wire that was threaded through a needle. Nine months after the port placement, a piece of broken wire was found in the patient's chest. An x-ray after the port was placed showed no broken wire in the chest. Apparently, someone tried to unstep the plastic catheter by threading a wire through a #18 gauge needle that had been stuck into the port. A cardiologist removed the wire without incident but the patient remained in the hospital overnight for observation. The complaint said that the Licensee abandoned her because he did not visit her while she was in the hospital. It was three or four months after the wire was removed that the Licensee learns of it. Another investigation that took longer than O.J.'s trial.

The letter to the "Licensee" further states that, if there is a hearing, at that time the Licensee will then be granted due process. The Constitution does not say that citizens will be granted due process when there is a hearing. The Constitution says that citizens will be granted due process, period. Perhaps "Licensees" aren't citizens.

The letter to the "Licensee" further states that at the time of the hearing, the "Licensee" may then cross-examine the complainant, if the complainant decides to show up. This clearly violates the Fifth Amendment and Pointer v. State of Texas Supreme Court 1960, which says that one is entitled to cross-examine witnesses against him.

Pain

There is a new doctor among us, the pain management specialist, re-treaded anesthesiologist, i.e. pain doctors, legal pushers. Perhaps our leaders, the insurance cartel, like pain doctors because the pain doctors can stick needles in the patients in an outpatient setting, thus saving an expensive hospital admission.

A "pain doctor" in Houston is building an eight million dollar house. Pain is Big Business.

After suturing a three suture cut on a child, Medicaid Mom says, "Watcha gonna give him for pain?" Maybe Mom takes or sells the pills. Nothing Mom – give the child aspirin.

Many years ago, at Charity Hospital of LA in New Orleans – if built today it would probably have to be named Entitlement Hospital of LA – had about forty operating rooms. There were only a few doctors with narcotic numbers to write narcotic prescriptions. Then, of course, we didn't have day surgery, laminectomies and drive-by mastectomies – nevertheless, patients didn't go home with a bottle full of Vicodin.

Pain medicine has been over-marketed and it is now winding up on the street and in our high schools. Junior takes some of Mom's pain pills to school.

"Sicko" is Sicko

I saw most of Michael Moore's Democratic, government medicine propaganda movie, Sicko. I certainly agree that the insurance oligarchs are not giving the people the insurance for which they paid, but instead the oligarchs are keeping their money for their salaries, bonuses and stock options.

We already have universal health care. The EMTALA Law allows everyone to show up at a hospital emergency room and be treated regardless of ability to pay. City/county or state charity hospitals take care of the indigent. The problem is the people above the poverty level who won't buy or can't afford to buy health insurance. Many had rather buy phones, cars, cigarettes, and booze. The answer is to cut out the waste and stealing and thus make health care affordable – not a health care system administered by the government – paid for maybe but administered by, never.

Regarding the Canadian golfer in Florida who ruptured his biceps tendon. Perhaps, if the Canadian golfer hadn't had his right thumb down the shaft of the club, he would not have had enough right hand in his swing to rupture his biceps tendon. Biceps tendons don't need repairing in older people.

Mr. Moore also failed to mention that in Canada and Great Britain, one has to wait several years for a hip replacement as well as other elective procedures. Great Britain also has an age limit for dialysis for chronic renal failure. Here, dialysis costs 40-50 thousand a year and there is no age limit as low as 55.

Canadian doctors work ten months a year or a few weeks a month or a few days a week. Our gross national product is the total of all of our goods and services produced.

It appears that a disproportionate number of new drugs and innovations come from the USA. It is not because of socialism.

Free Medicine

There is no such thing as a free lunch! The elderly in this country have been sold a "bill of goods" when it comes to the Medicare drug program. Ads on TV by movie stars, telemarketing and sales pitches by pharmacists have herded these old people into these programs. While in the doctor's waiting room, an elderly lady's cell phone rang. She answered it and was heard telling the person calling to stop calling her about signing up for the Medicare drug program.

Sometimes the elderly don't know that they (he) has been enrolled in the Medicare drug program.

They receive a letter from the government telling them that if a letter is not written by March, you cannot get out of the program for a year. Writing a letter is beyond the capability of many of the elderly people.

When a pensioner signs up for the Medicare Drug program, he loses much of what he already has under the existing Medicare program.

In all but about three of the sixty or so Medicare drug programs, can a patient continue to see his doctor that has been treating him for years? The remainder are put into an HMO (Health Maintenance Organization) owned by the insurance cartel and administered by the Fat-cat Republicans whose obscene multimillion dollar salaries, stock options and bonuses get even larger.

The HMO assigns the enrollee a doctor, other than the doctor who has been treating the enrollee for years and who knows the enrollees problems. The doctor's office may be across town. One elderly lady's doctor's office was across the street from a bus stop. The new doctor's office was not on a bus route. Uncle Sugar also doesn't bother to tell the enrollee that Medicare will no longer pay for home health or for nursing home care. The HMO fat cats get fatter off the backs of the poor and the elderly.

Many Medicare patients come to see his doctor not knowing that Medicare will not pay his doctor. The doctor will probably continue treating the patient until the patient can get out of the Medicare drug program.

The Medicare drug program has not caught up with the computer. Therefore, when a Medicare patient comes to the hospital, his insurance coverage cannot be confirmed. The doctor and the hospital don't get paid – the government and the HMO Fat-cats do.

Many of the elderly diabetic patients need home health visits to make sure that the patient gets his insulin. Twenty percent of the Medicare money is spent on diabetes. Controlling diabetes prevents arterial disease (strokes, heart attacks, gangrenous feet, kidney failure and blindness). Therefore, it is not cost effective to do away with home health for diabetics.

The answer to the expensive medicine problem is cheaper (more efficiently manufactured and distributed) medicine. This is difficult to accomplish with bankrupting class action lawsuits hanging over the heads of the pharmaceutical companies and the 1.4 billion dollars needed to test and bring a new drug to market.

Katrina

Houston opened its heart for the victims of Hurricane Katrina. It also opened the wallets of the U.S. taxpayers and the renters in Houston. For several decades, Houston has been run by real estate – shall we call them entrepreneurs? When an apartment renter's lease was up, due to supply and demand, the rent was increased. Vacant apartments and vacant motel rooms – at increased rates perhaps – were also rented.

Initially, the hurricane victims were housed in the Astrodome. When the place became dirty (trashed out), it was necessary to go to the day labor place and hire some illegal aliens, undocumenteds, to clean up the place for Senator Hillary and President Big George's photo-op hugging the children. The able-bodied hurricane victims were out spending their FEMA checks on crack and hos perhaps.

Medical care was provided for the victims. One woman with a toothache was taken by ambulance ten miles across the county to a small hospital emergency room. She was given pain pills and antibiotic pills and sent (by taxi) back to the Astrodome with instructions to see the dentist in the morning. She arrived by red taxi and returned by yellow taxi. The red taxi (ambulance) cost the taxpayers about $800-$1,200, the yellow taxi about $40. The emergency room visit was not cheap. There are other stories of ambulances taking patients from the Astrodome to ERs.

Mayor White received an award for the way he handled the Katrina disaster. From whom did this honor come?-The real estate entrepreneurs, the hospital entrepreneurs, the ambulance entrepreneurs.

Diabetes

Twenty percent of Medicare money is spent on diabetes. This probably includes complications of diabetes: gangrenous feet, strokes, end-stage renal disease and heart attacks.

Diabetes is divided into two groups: insulin dependent and non-insulin dependent diabetes. At present, insulin dependent diabetes may not be preventable. Adult onset or non-insulin dependent diabetes is another story.

Middle age people gradually put on weight and become more sedentary. Hypertension follows, then diabetes, then heart attacks, strokes and renal failure.

It is pretty much agreed that the better one controls one's diabetes, the fewer complications one has. Many of the diabetic complications are in the poor segment of our society. Perhaps because the poor are not smart enough to control their diabetes, can't afford correct food, can't afford medicine or all of the above.

Early education on nutrition and exercise would help. President Clinton is working to control obesity in children, but as strong as President Clinton's verbiage may be, it may not be strong enough to overcome the billions spent on advertising by the fast food and by the soft drink corporations.

Perhaps the government could offer a fifty million dollar tax-free reward to anyone who could transplant insulin producing cells without immuno-suppressing the patient. "Curing" diabetes would save much suffering and many resources.

Ambulances

The EMTALA Law (Emergency Medical Treatment and Active Labor Act) and the fear of litigation have turned our ambulances into taxis – expensive taxis, charging $800 to $1200 a trip. The Houston city ambulances, operated by the fire department have been instructed to pick up everyone who calls.

Many of our entitlees and non-resource citizens have caught on to this policy. The following are some of the more flagrant abuses of the taxpayers' money - $300 a year is added to the property taxes on our house for ambulances. The rest of the tab is picked up by U.S. taxpayers in general, through Medicare, Medicaid and perhaps increased insurance premiums.

Ambulance brings young dude to a small hospital emergency room. He has had flu symptoms for a week. He gets up off the stretcher and walks to sign in.

Drunk citizen calls ambulance from McDonald's because he ran out of his antacid medicine and has had stomach pains for one week and he vomited two hours ago. Lab and x-rays were normal. Patient had neither insurance nor money.

Dude with cap on backwards arrived in ER walking behind ambulance emergency medical technician (EMT).

A 210 pound, 15 year old girl gets punched in the face at school. She has a small abrasion under one eye without swelling. An ambulance brings her to the ER.

A three year old drops a can of apple juice on her big toe. Am ambulance brings her to the ER.

This foolishness must stop before it bankrupts us all.

A recent newspaper article said that the City of Houston was going to have a nurse on call to talk to people who called an ambulance. One does not need a nurse to tell one that he does not need an ambulance to bring a child who dropped a can of juice on his toe to the hospital or some man who had a urethral discharge for two weeks.

With regards to malpractice suits, treating patients by phone is hazardous. Most children have been vaccinated against a couple of bacteria that cause meningitis, but a snotty-nosed child with fever might have meningitis and be deaf in the morning. This plan has the potential of making some lawyers as rich as Senator Edwards.

HIPA

The Health Insurance Portability and Accountability Act has something to do with transferring ones insurance. The Health Insurance Portability and Accountability (HIPA) Law also deals with patients privacy.

A semi-private (semi-public) hospital room is usually defined as a hospital room with two beds in it. Our Texas State Board of Medical Examiners fined a doctor for talking so loud to a patient in a semi-private room that the family of the patient in the other bed overheard the doctor.

There was a hospitalized patient who spoke only Spanish. The doctor spoke less than perfect Spanish. When the family member did not want the responsibility of interpreting, it was necessary to call the government's interpreter hot line for several hundred dollars.

Recently, while quail hunting in South Texas, Vice President Cheney put some bird shot in his lawyer hunting partner – a not uncommon occurrence in South Texas quail hunts.

One might fault the hostess for having three hunters instead of two in the group but then, who is going to tell the Vice President what to do?

Senator Clinton screamed (screeched) that there was a "cover-up" because it was not immediately announced that Vice President Cheney had shot some bird shot into his lawyer, friend and colleague.

"Cover-up" among politicians is about as bad as beating ones mother.

It is against the HIPA Law that Senator Clinton and/or her husband passed to divulge medical information about a patient – or was it passed later?

Technically, perhaps the victim was not a patient until the ambulance arrived. Maybe Vice President Cheney should have called the press before he called the ambulance and it could have circumvented Senator Clinton's HIPA Law.

Patients are certainly entitled to privacy but the HIPA Law is not only burdensome but it is also expensive.

When Cho-Seung Hui bought a gun, he was supposed to fill out a federal form asking if the purchaser of a gun has a mental disorder. Because of the HIPA Law, the accuracy of a gun purchasers statement as to his mental health cannot be checked – thus a massacre at Virginia Tech.

The health care writers lament the waste of resources doing duplicate lab work. It is easier to repeat the lab work than to have the patient fill our papers and carry them to the hospital and get his lab work. A fax would probably go to the wrong fax machine. Heck, we got paid for repeating the tests anyway.

A patient calls his doctor at night. The doctor sends the patient to an emergency room. The emergency room doctor does tests and thinks that the patient does not require admission to the hospital but needs checking by his doctor the next morning. The doctor can't call the hospital and get the results of the tests done the night before.

When a patient is transferred from a smaller hospital emergency room to a larger hospital, one cannot get a follow-up in order to learn something because of the HIPA Law.

One pays for his eighteen year old son to go to a psychologist in Texas. The psychologist cannot give the results to the parents without the eighteen year old's permission.

Parents send an eighteen year old to college. They can't get the grades to see of their son or daughter needs some extra tutoring.

As a general rule, everything that the government does is counter productive.

The Privacy Act has some good spots but the insurance companies seem to get around the law.

Insurance

The insurance cartel, along with its fellow traveling lawyers, has ruined our country. Forty years ago, malpractice insurance for a general surgeon was $600. It increased to about $50,000. Cardiovascular (heart) surgeons were paying $100,000. That is $48-$50 an hour for a forty hour work week. The plaintiff (patient) gets about 17% of the malpractice premiums, therefore, the more the premiums, the more the insurance cartel makes.

The cartel can increase the premiums, because it pays claims and defends lawsuits. The cartel increases its expenses by settling lawsuits after its lawyers have run up big bills with motions and endless depositions. No matter what, the cartel and the lawyers get over 80% of the premiums.

As the TV hucksters say, "But wait, there is more." The doctors and the hospitals to prevent lawsuits or to better defend themselves, have resorted to defensive medicine, i.e. more tests, more consultants, more hospital admissions. Now the defensive medicine has morphed into maximizing income by the doctors and by the hospitals, increasing the costs even more.

The malpractice suits also involve the hospitals, resulting in larger hospital bills, which results in larger health insurance and workman's compensation insurance premiums. Companies pay much of the increased health insurance premiums, adding to their cost of doing business, making the company less competitive in world markets. To avoid this, the company might move out of the country. Medicare and Medicaid pay the increased doctor, hospital and pharmaceutical costs, which is "paid" by the taxpayers.

All businesses suffer the same fate as the health care business. A number of years ago, in the Midwest, a crosswalk at a hotel collapsed, killing and injuring a number of people. Over a hundred and fifty different entities were sued, resulting in increased liability premiums for all – and an increase cost of doing business for all. Because the insurance cartel and its lawyers get 80% of the premiums, they got fatter.

The insurance cartel which runs the Medicaid, HMOs (Health Maintenance Organization) pays the doctors so little that the doctors will lose money doing a procedure – thus the doctors won't do the procedures or they will go broke. Example: $350 for a carpal tunnel operation (cutting the bands on the front of the wrist because the band compresses the median nerve, causing pain in the hand. For $350, the doctor has to drive to the hospital and endure all of the obligatory fooling around attended with doing an operation: examine the patient, dictate the exam, talk to the family, wash his hands, wait for the anesthesiologist to deaden the arm, prep and drape the hand, do the procedure, dictate the operation, write the orders, talk to the family, change clothes and drive back to the office where the 40-50% overhead clock has been ticking. It is not worth it. The patient's hand keep hurting and the insurance oligarchs get fatter.

If a patient is seen in the doctor's office one day and is scheduled for surgery the next day, the patient is sent to the hospital to fill out admission papers, but the hospital won't do the necessary pre-operative studies until permission is granted by the insurance company. The doctor's office does not want to make the patient sit in the waiting room for an hour or two while permission is obtained for the operation. The patient then is required to get the pre-op studies the morning of the operation. If some of the studies are abnormal, an ECG and further evaluation is required, then the operation is cancelled, leaving a vacancy in the surgery scheduled. If the surgery schedule cannot be rearranged, then four or five employees plus the doctor and his assistant can drink coffee for a couple of hours.

The insurance cartel also squeezes the hospitals by paying only a percentage of their bill. If the bill goes over a certain amount, the cartel will pay a little more. It, therefore, is to the hospital's advantage to increase the charges and to pad the bills.

Doctors have to hire clerical staff help just to deal with insurance companies. The doctor has to get permission to treat the patient, has to file insurance claims, and in many cases refile insurance claims.

Many people are falsely insured. The patient thinks that he is insured but the insurance cartel denies his claim – pre-existing etc. If it is a hospital bill, the hospital wants the full amount of the bill rather than the 20% or so that the insurance cartel would pay. The high school drop-outs at the insurance company offices allegedly get bonuses for denying claims.

Hospitals require doctors to have malpractice insurance to work in the hospital. Putting the doctors at the mercy of the insurance cartel. This is involuntary servitude, because the hospitals are making the doctors buy insurance for the hospitals.

Very few doctors do minor office surgery. The thirty-five dollars that the insurance cartel pays for removing a mole or a sebaceous cyst barely covers the cost of the material necessary to do the minor procedure. Many doctors remove the bumps in an outpatient surgery setting at many times the cost and much wasted time for the doctor.

Because of enormous malpractice premiums doctors cannot slow down, work part time or do fewer operations. A doctor has to work full steam to pay his insurance premiums or quit. An ophthalmologist sold his practice and wanted to stay on and just do office practice – no surgery. He couldn't because of malpractice premiums. Retired doctors might want to donate their services to a charity clinic. They can't because of malpractice premiums. The insurance cartel has seen to it that the services of a number of able bodied doctors are being wasted.

The government has tried to herd everybody into HMOs (Health Maintenance Organizations) owned and operated by the insurance cartel. State Medicaid patients have been put in HMOs. Some Medicare patients that signed up for the Medicare drug program have been put in HMOs. Texas Children's Hospital, one of the best hospitals in the country, will not accept children covered by the HMO Americaid. Texas Children's Hospital will, however, accept children with no resources. The HMO Evercare (Nevercare) pays so little that many doctors won't accept it.

Conclusion

Senator Clinton has a health care plan, Senator Obama has a health care plan but no one has defined health care, said how much it will cost, nor addressed the inefficiency and the fraud that now is occurring.

General Motors signed a contract giving retired workers "health care" not knowing what health care entailed, nor how much it cost. Little did GM know how much the health care providers could steal. Is our government going to do the same?

Is health care allowing entitlees to use ambulances as taxis? Is health care allowing an entitlee to go to an ER for an infected submaxillary gland, receive antibiotic pills, take one or two of them and go to another emergency room the next day? Is health care allowing Medicaid moms to bring their child to an ER instead of to a doctor's office, costing the taxpayers twenty times as much? Is health care allowing a Medicare patient to recall an ambulance to return her to the ER because the ER doctor forgot to put his narcotic number on her prescription? The pharmacist could have called. Is health care the EMTALA Law (Emergency Medical Treatment and Active Labor Act) that allows anyone, anytime, for anything to go to any hospital emergency room and be examined and stabilized, regardless of their ability to pay.

There are now forty to fifty million uninsured people in the U.S. They are either too rich to go to a charity hospital or to get Medicaid or they are too poor to afford the exorbitant health insurance premiums. I hope that our health care planners will not put these forty to fifty million people on the Medicaid rolls without first controlling the waste and fraud that the entitlees and their providers are now able to heap upon the taxpayers.

Any systems predicated on the honesty, the integrity, and the altruism of the participants will either fail or be expensive beyond reason, as General Motors found out.

If anyone wants the federal government to administer health care, he should stand in line at the post office or at the passport office. No matter how inefficient a federal agency, it can't go bankrupt because the federal government will just print more money.

Capitalism and free markets mean efficiency. One of our greatest freedoms is the freedom to go broke. Anyone is free to open a business. Health care is a business. If Walmart can provide better, more efficient (cheaper) health care, then let them do so.

The standard of living of a country depends on the productivity of the people – except here in the U.S. where we print money and pay Chinamen to produce things for us. We still pay by inflation increasing the cost of things we buy and by diminishing the value of our savings.

Health care is a business hiring, nine million people or 8% of the total workforce. Health care, therefore, is a big business. Except for having Indians read x-rays by teleradiology and having foreigners make medical machines and pharmaceuticals, most health care is done by Americans – native born and naturalized.

Chris Farrell in his book, "Deflation", quotes Robert Snorbus who said, regarding business, "You have to be more productive and get costs out that aren't contributing to that productivity."

Well, health care is a business, and lawyers, while preventing some patient abuse, don't contribute to productivity. Lawyers don't contribute to the productivity of any business. General Motors has hundreds of thousands of lawsuits against it, Toyota doesn't.

The EMTALA (Emergency Medical Treatment and Active Labor Act) must be repealed. This law now allows the patients, the hospitals, the ambulances and the doctors to waste a monumental amount of the taxpayer's money.

The insurance companies should be put under the antitrust law if this has not been done. The insurance oligarchs should not be allowed to steal so much of the taxpayer's money, while not providing the patient's the care for which the oligarchs had been paid to provide.

Relief from malpractice litigation, fear of malpractice litigation (defensive medicine), which has now morphed into maximizing income by doctors and hospitals must be contained. The malpractice crisis is caused by a symbiotic relationship between the insurance cartel and the lawyers. There cannot be a significant lawsuit without a rich defendant or an insured defendant. Poor people are judgment proof.

The doctors are stealing, the lawyers are stealing, the hospitals are stealing, the insurance cartel is stealing, the ambulance companies are stealing and the patients are stealing. Some of the stealing is fraud, others are just maximizing income. It must stop.

The colonists got tired of supporting King James' lifestyle, threw his tea into Boston Harbor and started a revolution. The French peasants get tired of supporting King Louie's lavish lifestyle, revolted and lopped off the last King Louie's head with a guillotine. The Russian peasants got tired of supporting the lavish lifestyle of the Czars, revolted and got their boy Lenin to kill the czar and his entire family.

Today, the political leaders have breached their Fiduciary Duty to the taxpayers by allowing the doctors, the lawyers, the hospitals, the insurance cartel and the patients to waste and steal the taxpayer's money. It is time that the taxpayers revolted at the polls and throw off this onerous health care cost burden, caused by bad laws, lack of oversight and curtailment of free market forces.

Dr. McGuire, CEO of United Health Care that administers Medicaid HMOs, 1.7 billion dollars in unexercised stock options is no less obscene that Katherine the Great's fifteen thousand dresses.

Senator Clinton found out what happens when one tries to cut the insurance cartel out of the loop, as she did when her husband was president. Now she sings a different tune. Our country is neither a democracy nor a federation but it is a corporate oligarchy. Perhaps nothing can be done to dislodge the insurance oligarchs.

Our country probably is better off being run by corporate oligarch than being run by an eighth grade electorate, but the insurance oligarchs have stolen so much that, due to medical and liability insurance premiums, our corporations can no longer compete on world markets.

In Texas, there has been some progress made in cost containment. A constitutional amendment limiting damages for pain and suffering to $250,000 was passed. Economic damages were unaffected. This constitutional amendment has prevented many unmeritorious lawsuits.

Several years ago, an informed consent law was passed requiring the complications that could occur with certain operations be listed and signed by the doctor as well as by the patient. This prevented lawsuits unless both lawyers were on the same side – theirs, not yours.

Recently, in Texas, experts in medical malpractice suits had to have a Texas license and had to be an expert in the field in which the alleged malpractice occurred. This prevents the retired, doting old fools, living in Sun City who advertise in the Bar Journals from coming to town and saying that which the plaintiff lawyer paid him to say.

The city/county (charity) hospital now requires non-emergency patients who come to the emergency room to pay $25 if they want to be seen at that time. Otherwise, the patient is given an appointment to the clinic for the next day.

Hospitals are now putting charts and x-rays on computers. Radiologists can now read x-rays from home or from halfway around the world. Robots now deliver drugs to the nurses' station. Nurse practitioners now see patients and assist in surgery.

Medicare recently said that Medicare would no longer pay for self-referrals, i.e. doctors sending patients to their own facilities or machines.

It is an economic law that if things are too cheap, there will be a scarcity. If things are too expensive, there will be a surplus. Medicaid patients can't get plastic surgeons to do skin grafts and close bedsores. One has to wait years for a hip replacement in Great Britain. Canadians are having trouble finding a primary care doctor – free but unavailable. On the other hand, when doctors received $3,000 and hospitals received about $30,000 for a "fat operation", one probably could get on the surgery schedule in the morning.

What kind of health care system do we need? Private insurance as we now have? Medicare, as we now have? Employers, paying for employees, only companies should be able to deal directly with hospitals, clinics and doctors without going through an insurance company if the company chooses to do so. Medicaid, with better cost control over the entitlees and the insurance oligarchs.

Everyone should be entitled to basic health care. If one wants a private room and lobster for dinner, he could pay for it.

Let the insurance companies, clinics, hospitals and other entities compete to take care of the forty to fifty million uninsured. The taxpayers, as well as the uninsured, could pay for it.

The waste, fraud and inefficiency in our present as well as any future system must be addressed.

Patients are admitted to the hospital under a diagnostic code. Perhaps the best doctors in the country – not just the "dog and frog doctors" from the medical schools, but also by doctors practicing in the community, could devise a computer printout giving the latest information on the disease represented by the diagnostic code and the best method of treating it. This printout could be put on the chart for nurses and doctors to read. If the doctor was not negligent in other ways and if the doctor followed the guidelines, the patient would be barred from suing the doctor and the hospital.

But, you say, this is already the law – a doctor is not liable if he meets the standard of care. It doesn't work that way here in Harris County (Houston) Texas, the epicenter of malpractice litigation. Consultants, anesthesiologists, nurse anesthesiologist, surgical assistant, surgeons who corrected the mishap, along with his assistant and the doctor who referred the patient have been sued.

A letter to the editor in the Financial Times said that no U.S. doctor had ever been sued for ordering too many CT scans or lab work and I might add that no U.S. doctor has been sued for calling in too many consultants who ordered too many CT scans and too much lab work.

Larry Mellon, at the age of forty, entered Tulane Medical School, graduated in about 1952, bought the Standard Fruit Plantation in Haiti and built a hospital there. It cost Larry about $600,000 a year to operate the hospital. The doctors and the nurses were lined up and the patients were lined up to be treated. There were no reams of papers to be filled out, the Haitians spoke a patois that was an unwritten language. There was no hall lined with offices for CEOs, COOs, CFOs, nursing directors, infection control nurses, quality assurance nurses, case managers and business offices – Larry and his wife, Gwen, ran the place.

Today, $600,000 would pay only a fraction of the liability insurance in a hospital and outpatient clinic of that size.

Years ago, the charity hospitals in Louisiana, Cook Country and Los Angeles County and others were similar institutions where doctors and nurses took care of patients. There were no reams of papers to fill out nor offices full of non-nursing nurses, whose only function was to avoid liability suits.

Times have changed, but doctors and nurses still take care of patients. It seems that there is a lot of fat that could be cut out of our present system.

If administrative costs are 22% of the two trillion health care tab (three hundred billion) then this seems to be an area where money could be saved. Much that does not add to productivity is done by hospitals, doctors and companies to avoid litigation: nurses to fill out bed sore sheets every shift, quality assurance nurses, infection control nurses and case manager nurses along with endless hospital committee meetings.

Doctors are forced to have a clerical staff to deal with insurance companies. The staff has to hang on the phone sometimes for up to an hour to get permission to treat a patient or to get paid for treating a patient.

Insurance claims are denied and have to be refilled for various reasons: wrong birthday, pre-existing, wrong address, etc.

I have done probably thirty to fifty Medicaid cholecystectomys, for which I wasn't paid. Some due to my incompetent office staff, perhaps. If the claims aren't refilled within a certain period, the claims won't be paid.

On one occasion, a claim was denied because the claim was sent to the wrong address. When the new address was obtained, it was the same old address. Oops, too late, you should have refilled it sooner.

According to the Wall Street Journal, 1.4 million workers make 700,000 cars in a Russian state run auto company. One hundred thirty thousand workers make 2.5 million cars in Fiat Company plants.

When devising a health care system, advantage should be taken of the capitalistic free market system that has made our great nation what it is today. Socialism does not work.

www.ingramcontent.com/pod-product-compliance
Lightning Source LLC
Chambersburg PA
CBHW081227170526
45165CB00009B/2990